Unicorn
wishes

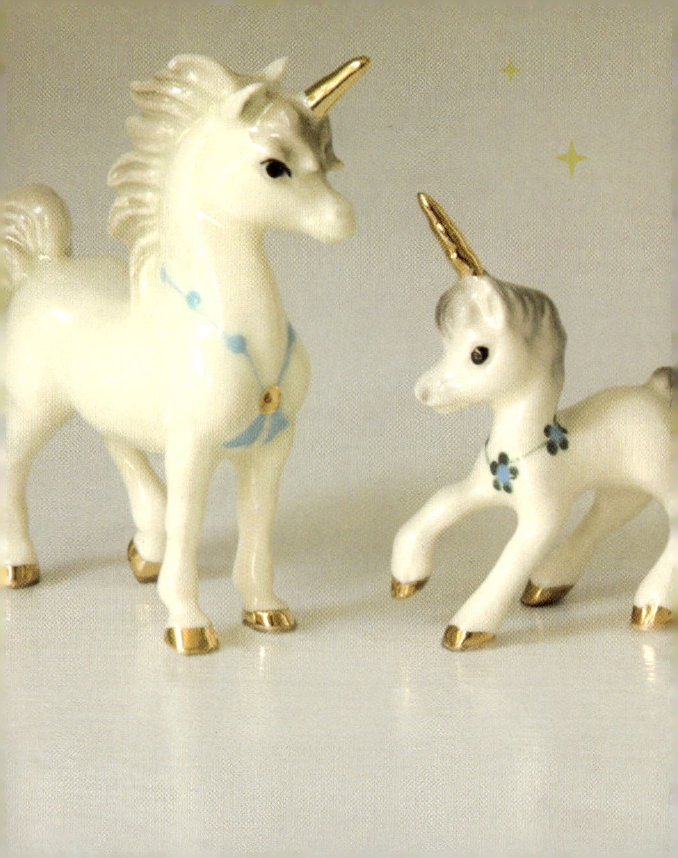

Unicorn wishes

By Micaela Heekin

CHRONICLE BOOKS
SAN FRANCISCO

Text copyright © 2009 by Chronicle Books LLC.
Illustrations copyright © 2009 by Stanley Martucci.

All rights reserved. No part of this book
may be reproduced in any form without
written permission from the publisher.

Illustration on page 7: Courtesy of Oberlin College
Library Special Collections.

Illustration on page 23: The Metropolitan Museum
of Art, Gift of John D. Rockefeller Jr., 1937 (37.80.6)
Image © The Metropolitan Museum of Art.

ISBN 978-0-8118-6715-3

Manufactured in China.
Design by Suzanne LaGasa.
Photographs by Alexis Tjian.
Typeset in Magic Spell and Eureka.

Chronicle Books endeavors to use
environmentally responsible paper
in its gift and stationery products.

10 9 8 7 6 5 4 3 2 1

Chronicle Books LLC
680 Second Street
San Francisco, CA 94107

www.chroniclebooks.com

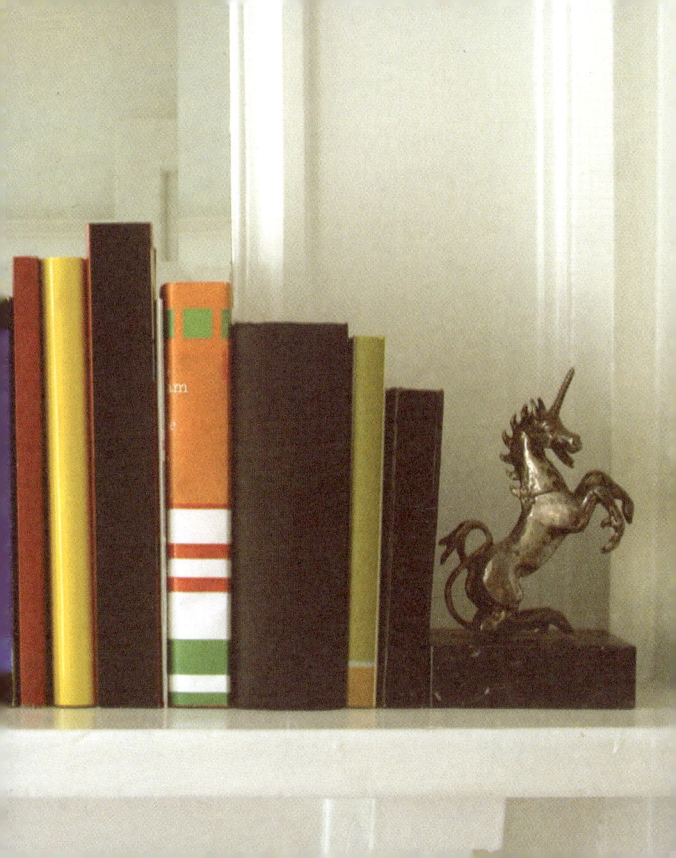

When You Wish Upon a Unicorn All Your Dreams Come True!

EVERYONE LOVES UNICORNS.

These beautiful and mysterious creatures have captured the popular imagination for centuries. The belief in their mystical powers and abilities—and in their very existence—has a long and storied past. Depicted in the art, folklore, and literature of diverse world cultures, from ancient times through the Middle Ages and into the present day, unicorns have been thought to possess magical qualities.

Unicorns are described differently in various regions across the globe—including Europe, China, and India—as small as a goat or as large as an elephant, with mixed features of the horse, deer, lion, goat, and antelope. Though in their contemporary depiction they are generally white in color, they have also traditionally been rendered in a range of equine and even rainbow colors. The one consistent feature throughout is that of a single horn protruding from the middle of their foreheads. The horn can vary in size, shape (straight or spiral), and color. Unicorns are generally believed to be powerful yet gentle, pure, and solitary creatures. Although these accounts can differ greatly from each other, they all point to the unicorn's identity as a fantastical beast that has played a significant and symbolic role in the myths and legends of different world cultures for thousands of years.

CHINESE LEGENDS DESCRIBE the existence of the unicorn as early as 2800 B.C., the time of the legendary emperor Fu Hsi, whose reign reportedly marked the introduction of writing, hunting, and fishing to Chinese civilization. Legend holds that, while the emperor was walking beside the Yellow River and pondering the impermanent nature of life and how to record his thoughts for future generations, he was visited by a unicorn that had markings on its body. From these markings the emperor established the fundamentals of written Chinese language, and so the unicorn is credited with bringing this great gift to the Chinese people.

In Chinese mythology, the unicorn is considered to be one of the four superior creatures—along with the tortoise, the phoenix, and the dragon—that were believed to foretell future events and represent good omens. The Chinese unicorn, called *k'i-lin* (a combination of the male *ki* and female *lin* single-horned creatures), appears in many different forms, but the most common is that of a beast with the body of a deer (sometimes with the head of a lion), the hooves of a horse, and the tail of an ox. The k'i-lin's coat contains the five sacred Chinese colors (red, yellow, blue, white, and black), and its call is musical in nature. Its appearance is believed to be a harbinger of good things to come: A k'i-lin is said to have appeared to Confucius's mother before the great scholar was born. Thereafter, Chinese mothers often put images of unicorns on their walls in order to influence their unborn children's wisdom, and the Chinese gods who were thought to oversee the births of children were often depicted riding k'i-lin.

It was a type of k'i-lin that saved India from invasion by the Mongolian warrior Genghis Khan in the thirteenth century. The unicorn appeared and knelt before Genghis Khan as he crested a mountain with his army, ready to conquer India. He took the unicorn's appearance to be a sign from heaven and turned back.

The unicorn in Japanese legend, known as the formidable *kirin* or *sin-you*, has a keen sense of justice and an ability to discern right from wrong. Accordingly, the kirin would be summoned to appear in court to sit in judgment of the accused. If the person was found guilty, the unicorn would pierce the accused's heart with a single blow from its horn. The Japanese unicorn is portrayed in different forms, but the most familiar has a bull's body, a lion's face, and dragon scales.

IN THE WESTERN WORLD, one of the earliest surviving written accounts of a unicorn is from 416 B.C. by the Greek historian and physician Ctesias. After an extended visit to Persia, where he heard many tales from travelers and merchants, Ctesias described an animal that looked like an ass with a single, multicolored horn growing from its head:

II

> *There are in India certain wild asses which are as large as horses, and larger. Their bodies are white, their heads dark red, and their eyes dark blue. They have a horn on the forehead which is about a foot and a half in length. The dust filed from this horn is administered in a potion as a protection against deadly drugs. The base of this horn . . . is pure white; the upper part is sharp and of a vivid crimson; and the remainder, or middle portion is black. Those who drink out of these horns, made into drinking vessels, are not subject, they say, to convulsions or the holy disease [epilepsy]. . . . The animal is exceedingly swift and powerful, so that no creature, neither the horse nor any other, can overtake it.*
>
> —Ctesias, *Indica* (quote from Odell Shepard's *The Lore of the Unicorn*)

The famous Greek philosopher Aristotle (384–322 B.C.), likely having read Ctesias's work, also mentions an "Indian ass" with a single horn growing from its head. It is said that he did not believe in the unicorn's magical qualities, but his recognition of its possible existence supported the belief in the unicorn as a real creature and not just a mythological concept.

In his book *The Gallic Wars*, Roman emperor Julius Caesar claimed to have seen single-horned creatures that appeared "like an ox shaped like a stag" in the Black Forest in Germany, where he spent time as a soldier in the first century B.C. (However, he described the horn as branching out at the top, more like a central antler than the classic single horn.) Pliny the Elder, the Roman naturalist who lived early in the first century A.D., wrote in his book *Historia Naturalis* of a "Monoceros" that had the body of a horse, the feet of an elephant, and a single long, black horn.

Though the physical descriptions of the unicorn differ, and sometimes sound suspiciously close to that of the single-horned rhinoceros, certain characteristics emerged as common across different cultures. Unicorns were usually considered solitary creatures and were rarely sighted and almost impossible to catch. These traits, often described by traders and travelers who claimed to have encountered the animals, also helped (perhaps conveniently) explain why it was so difficult to substantiate unicorn sightings. Though the creatures sounded fantastical, the goods that the traders brought home were equally exotic. To a woman who had never been exposed to fabrics other than her own rough, home-woven creations, the touch of silk would certainly feel otherworldly. It was a time of discoveries and strange encounters—so why not accept the idea of a mystical horse with a single horn?

While a mob of wallabies or a shiver of sharks might wander through the traders' stories, a herd of unicorns seldom appeared. The only sightings reported were of a single unicorn, and tradition held that attempts to capture one by force would always fail, as would any ordinary trap. It was only a young woman who possessed the purest nature (a virgin) who could attract a unicorn. If she went to a place where unicorns were believed to visit, eventually one would see her and be attracted to her purity. If she sat still long enough, the unicorn would come to her and sometimes even lay its head in her lap. The unicorn would remain tame and quiet for the maiden, and she would in turn summon the hunters who would then capture the beast.

IN INDIA, THE LEGEND OF THE UNICORN first appeared in the *Mahabharata*, an epic poem written in Sanskrit around 200 B.C. In the poem, a Hindu holy man withdraws from society and, after years of wandering alone, makes a home for himself beside the Kausiki River. While he is there, a beautiful doe comes to him and they fall in love. Months later, the doe gives birth to a baby boy with a horn growing from the middle of his head. They name him Risharinga, meaning "antelope horn." The doe dies soon after, and the boy's father is left to raise him alone. Many years go by, and the boy and his father live without interference from the outside world, self-sufficient and unaware of a drought that has affected the land and left people in the cities starving to death. The emperor, who has heard tales of the unicorn boy, dispatches his fair and virtuous young daughter to bring Risharinga to his palace with the hope that the enchanted boy will bring rain. The plan works, and the rains accompany the pair as they travel back to her father's kingdom, where they are then married.

The Arabian unicorn was called the *karkadann*, and

it differed from the more gentle subjects of other cultures' legends. Here the unicorn was a ferocious and potentially violent beast, as large as a rhinoceros, and able to kill an elephant with a blow from its single black horn. Legends describe Alexander the Great taming a karkadann and riding it into battle in the third century B.C

Legends of the German unicorn often took place around the Harz Mountains region of central Germany. One tale tells of a wise old woman who lived in the Steingrotte cave in the forest of this region. She would advise and heal those who visited her. When Christian missionaries denounced her as a witch and soldiers approached to arrest her, she rode away to safety on a unicorn that emerged from the cave.

In 1663, a unicorn skeleton was allegedly discovered in the Harz Mountains region in a cave called the Einhornhohle or Unicorn Cave. This supposed unicorn skeleton had only two legs, and at first was believed to be real, but upon further investigation it was evident that it had been fabricated from fossil bones of other animals.

THE UNICORN ALSO APPEARS in the King James version of the Bible, most likely because of a mistranslation of the word *re'em*, which meant "horned" in Hebrew. Between the second and third centuries B.C., Hebrew scholars translated the Old Testament into Greek, and in doing so replaced *re'em* with their word for single-horned creature, which was eventually translated into unicorn. In other translations, this same *re'em* has been translated as "wild ox," "monoceros," "einhorn," and other words for creatures with one horn.

Some attempts to discount theories about the unicorn's existence point to the fact that it wasn't named as one of the creatures that Noah took aboard his ark. A Jewish folktale clarifies this point by explaining that unicorns were demanding creatures, and because of the amount of space and attention they required, Noah banished them from the boat before the flood. So, according to this tale, it may have been a diva-like turn that kept them off the boat. (Some believers hold that after the flood, unicorns learned to live in a world of water and evolved into the single-horned whales called narwhals.)

For many, the appearance of the unicorn in the Bible proved that it was real. A Greek text known as the *Physiologus*, written sometime between A.D. 200 and 400, went even further to spread belief in the unicorn. The author was an anonymous Greek naturalist who, like Aesop, used stories about animals to teach moral lessons. The book covers a number of real and mythical animals, including the unicorn, the phoenix, and the manticore (a lion-like animal with the face of a human, blood-red eyes, and the tail of a scorpion). In the *Physiologus*, the unicorn is compared to Jesus Christ, and the text draws a parallel between the belief that only the purest young woman could approach the unicorn and the Virgin Birth. The text also indicates that the unicorn's horn was a physical manifestation of the unity between God and Jesus. The stories were very popular, and the *Physiologus* was translated into many different languages. Over the years the text grew to include more animals and is cited as the inspiration for the medieval bestiaries (collections of stories describing both real and chimerical animals).

The tales included in these bestiaries often had moral or symbolic significance. In one such tale from sometime in the twelfth through fourteenth centuries, a serpent would come to a river, a source of water shared by all animals, and poison the water—which could then only be purified by a unicorn dipping its horn into the water and thereby neutralizing the poison (another salvation parallel between the unicorn and Jesus Christ).

Unicorns played a prominent role in medieval ornamentation, as is evident in the decorative motifs on windows and in paintings in medieval churches and castles in Europe. They are often featured on drinking vessels and hand-washing basins used by the nobility and the clergy.

IN THE MIDDLE AGES, it was not uncommon for an upstart to rise to the throne by assassinating his predecessor, and poison, because it was so difficult to detect, was a murder weapon of choice. Unicorn horn—or substances presented as such—gained popularity as a purported antidote to poison. A horn, or a fragment of one, would sometimes be used as a dining table centerpiece and was believed to be seen "sweating" if poison was present. Kings and queens were given the horns as gifts, and at one point in the 1400s a unicorn's horn was valued at twice its weight in gold. Other uses for the horn included the curing of many physical ailments: A powdered unicorn horn was thought to cure smallpox and other deadly illnesses, and it was also used as a panacea for more common aches and pains.

Tests to authenticate a unicorn's horn were constantly being invented. Some experimenters would put scorpions inside the horn and then seal it off. If the scorpions were still alive hours later, the horn was declared a fake. Another test involved birds that, after being fed arsenic, were fed scraped-off bits of unicorn horn. If the birds lived, the horn was said to be genuine.

Due to its medicinal and magical qualities, the unicorn horn was a prize sought by nobility. One of the most famous depictions of unicorns to emerge from medieval times is a set of seven textiles known as the *Unicorn Tapestries*. The wall hangings, which are thought to have been woven in Brussels between 1495 and 1505 and now hang in the Cloisters museum in New York, tell the tale of a unicorn hunt from beginning to end. Noblemen, huntsmen, and hounds pursue an elusive unicorn; after the unicorn evades them, the hunters use a maiden to lure the unicorn, which is then captured, killed, and, in the last and most famous tapestry, reborn (the unicorn is alive and chained to a tree).

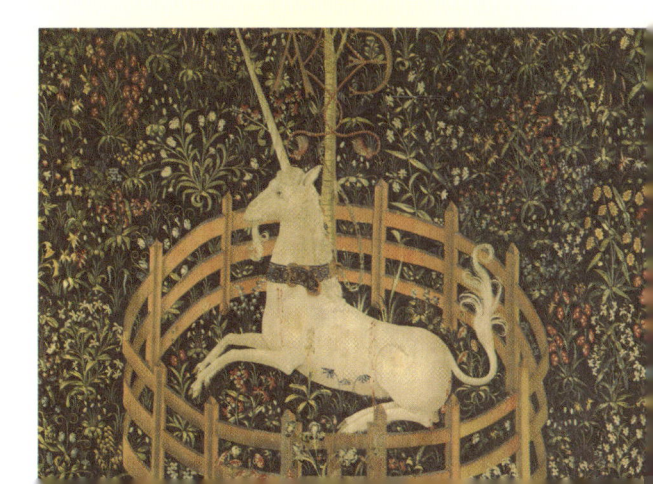

The tapestries are rich with symbolism and combine secular and religious themes. In one interpretation the unicorn is seen as Christ, the maiden as the Virgin Mary, the death of the unicorn as the crucifixion, and the last panel as the resurrection. According to another interpretation of these tapestries, which some scholars believe were a wedding gift, the unicorn represents a bridegroom, the rabbits (known for their reproductive vigor) signify a wish to conceive many children, and the tiny frog hidden in the grass plays the all-important role of aphrodisiac.

The unicorn plays a prominent role in another set of tapestries known as *The Lady and the Unicorn*, woven around A.D. 1500 and housed in the Musée de Cluny in Paris. Each of the six tapestries depicts a noble lady with a lion on her right and a unicorn on her left. One interpretation of these tapestries, like the theories regarding the *Unicorn Tapestries*, draws parallels between the virgin depicted and the Virgin Mary, and between the unicorn and Jesus Christ.

Unicorns became popular as heraldic motifs around the fifteenth century. Robert III, who took the throne of Scotland in 1390, had unicorns carved on either side of the door to his palace and also added them to the royal coat of arms. It's most likely that he chose the unicorn for its inability to be taken or tamed—the creature was seen as a symbol of power and virility. In a related vein, the English coat of arms was shown with lions supporting it, and an English nursery rhyme tells of the lion and unicorn fighting and chasing each other—a thinly veiled allusion to the constant struggles between England (the lion) and Scotland (the unicorn) for the crown. In 1603, when James VI of Scotland took the English throne after Elizabeth I's death, becoming King James I of England and Scotland, he replaced one of the lions on the English coat of arms with a unicorn, so that a lion now supports one side, and a unicorn supports the other.

Great Britain

THE RENAISSANCE IN EUROPEAN SOCIETY brought with it a turn for the scientific and the rational in the 1600s, and scientific treatises and essays were written attempting to prove and disprove the existence of unicorns. Europeans had known of the narwhal for centuries, and it became understood that narwhal horns were most likely the source for the many "unicorn horns" that were being bought and sold all over Europe. As a result, the narwhal's existence came to substantiate the unicorn's nonexistence. Belief in the unicorn, and depictions of them, soon dwindled in the West.

IN THE 1800S, renowned French naturalist and zoologist Georges Cuvier declared that unicorns existed merely in fairy tales. Although there had been debate and doubts cast on the unicorn's existence in the past, Cuvier's highly respected reputation, along with the rising popular faith in science, made the pronouncement stick. Cuvier referred to Pliny's *Historia Naturalis* in the basis for his argument, saying that cloven-hoofed creatures, such as the unicorn, must also have cloven skulls, thus making it impossible for the unicorn to grow a single horn from the center of its forehead.

However, in 1933, Dr. W. Franklin Dove, a professor from the University of Maine, undertook an experiment to prove that unicorns could physically exist by "creating" a unicorn; he surgically transplanted the horn buds of a day-old bull to the center of its head, where they fused together and grew into a single horn. Dove's experiment, which proved that a cloven-hoofed animal could indeed potentially grow a single horn, gave renewed faith to the true unicorn believers (though by that point, they were few and far between).

EVEN IF BELIEF in the unicorn's existence faded with the passage of time, this legendary beast has remained a prominent and symbolic figure in art and literature, well into the present day. Lewis Carroll's *Through the Looking Glass and What Alice Found There*(1871) includes a chapter titled "The Lion and the Unicorn," in which the two creatures fight for the crown. The unicorn beholds Alice and, thinking she is a "fabulous monster," approaches her:

> The Unicorn looked dreamily at Alice, and said, "Talk, child."
>
> Alice could not help her lips curling into a smile as she began: "Do you know, I always thought Unicorns were fabulous monsters, too! I never saw one alive before!"
>
> "Well, now that we have seen each other," said the Unicorn, "if you'll believe in me, I'll believe in you."
>
> —Lewis Carroll, *Through the Looking Glass and What Alice Found There*

In 1930, Odell Shepard wrote *The Lore of the Unicorn*, a comprehensive text tracing the development, evolution, and historical significance of unicorns in legend, folklore, and mythology.

In *The Last Battle*, the final book of C. S. Lewis's famous series *The Chronicles of Narnia* (1956), Peter, the oldest of the Pevensie siblings, leads the charge on the back of a noble unicorn. He emerges victorious, having freed Narnia and saved his brother Edmund.

Peter S. Beagle's book *The Last Unicorn* (1968), a

classic of fantasy literature that sold more than five million copies worldwide. This creature, warned by a hunter to stay deep in the forest because she is the last of her kind, sets out on a quest to find the truth about what happened to the rest of the unicorns. She encounters numerous interesting characters on her journey and eventually finds the unicorns and saves them from an unhappy fate.

In the 1960s and 1970s, a search for spirituality and meaning beyond materialism led to a renewed cultural interest in the natural and mythological realms. This period saw the rise of the New Age movement, mysticism, hippie culture, and fantasy themes in the popular culture. Fantastical creatures are featured prominently in J.R.R. Tolkien's *The Hobbit* and his *Lord of the Rings* series, which established its immense cult readership in the era. Similarly, the game *Dungeons and Dragons*, first released in 1974, also reignited interest in magical worlds populated with enchanted beasts. By the time people started airbrushing wizards on the sides of their vans, the world was ready to believe in unicorns again, or at least ready to embrace them as a symbol of purity, strength, gentle nature, and imagination. Unicorns were everywhere: on T-shirts, stickers, figurines, velvet paintings, and posters. They also appeared in context with some of the other optimistic symbols of the time, such as shooting stars and rainbows.

One of the strangest events in unicorn history happened in the late 1970s and early 1980s. A man named Oberon Zell-Ravenheart and his wife, Morning Glory, transplanted the horn buds on ten baby goats, fusing the horns together in the center of the goats' heads, much like Dr. Dove had done forty years earlier. Oberon and Morning Glory took the "unicorns" on tours to Renaissance fairs and leased four of them to Barnum and Bailey's circus; the most famous of the four was called "Lancelot." (All ten were named for the knights of the Round Table.)

Though the surgery had been performed before—a tribe in Africa had been performing it for centuries on their cattle—Zell-Ravenheart's purpose for performing it was unique. He and his wife practiced Paganism and believed, like many others had over the centuries, that the appearance of a unicorn was a sign of good things to come. They saw their efforts to create a unicorn as a way to bring a good omen and symbol of hope and purity to the world.

The ideal of the modern unicorn is the result of a combination of all the world's legends. The belief in the existence of unicorns outlasted the belief in many other mythical creatures that were once thought real, like the griffin, the centaur, and the fire-breathing dragon . . . Perhaps the unicorn's staying power lies in its beauty, purity, strength, and independence, as well as its elusive and mysterious nature.

How to Use This Set

Unicorns are symbols of hope and good luck, and fortunate indeed are those who possess one of their very own. Use this unicorn figure as a special talisman to symbolize what you value most deeply in your heart. Display your figurine close to you during the day to welcome good fortune into your life, or near your bed at night to allow the unicorn to watch over your dreaming life. Your unicorn is a powerful symbol and the key to a world where magic is real and wishes come true.

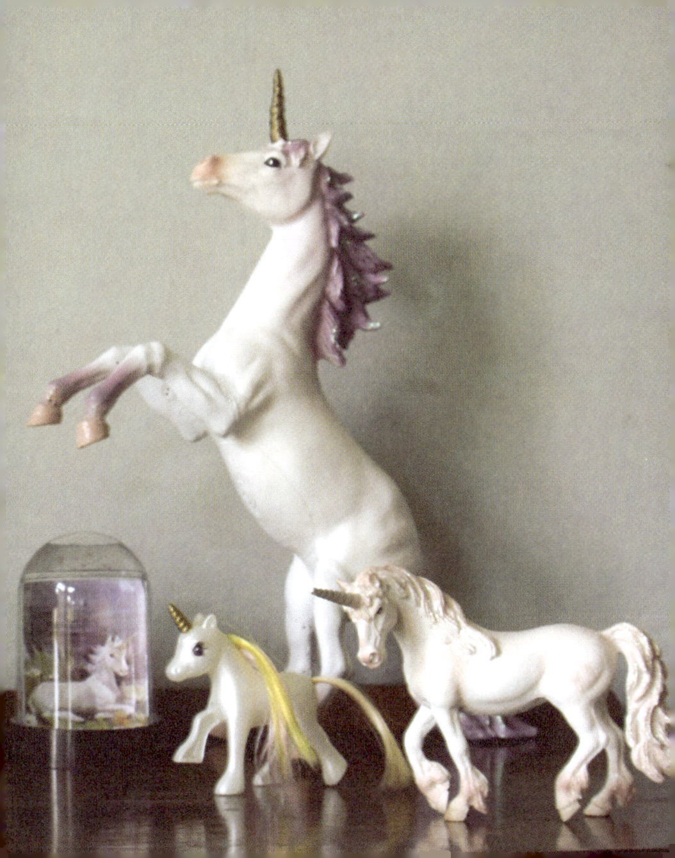

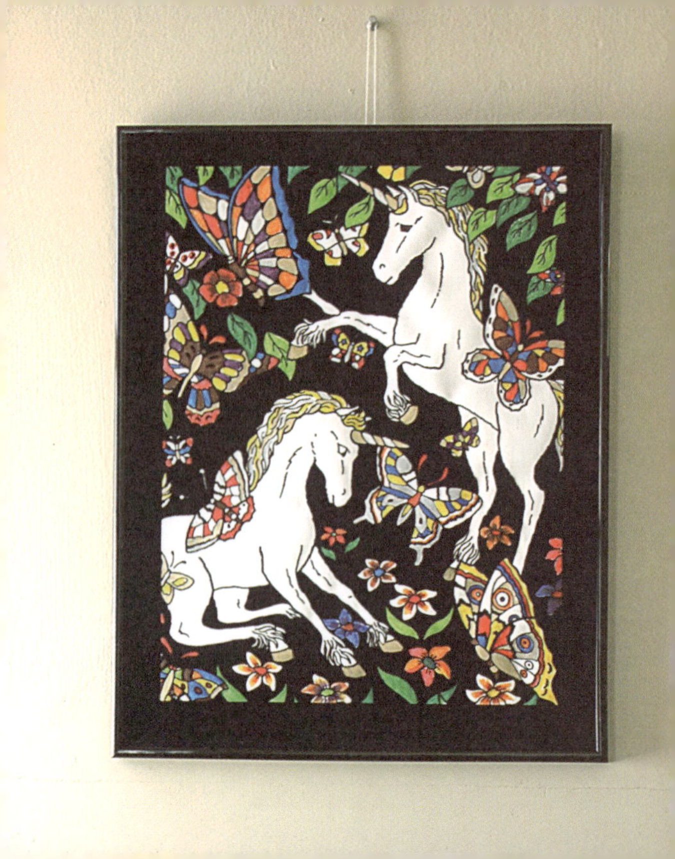

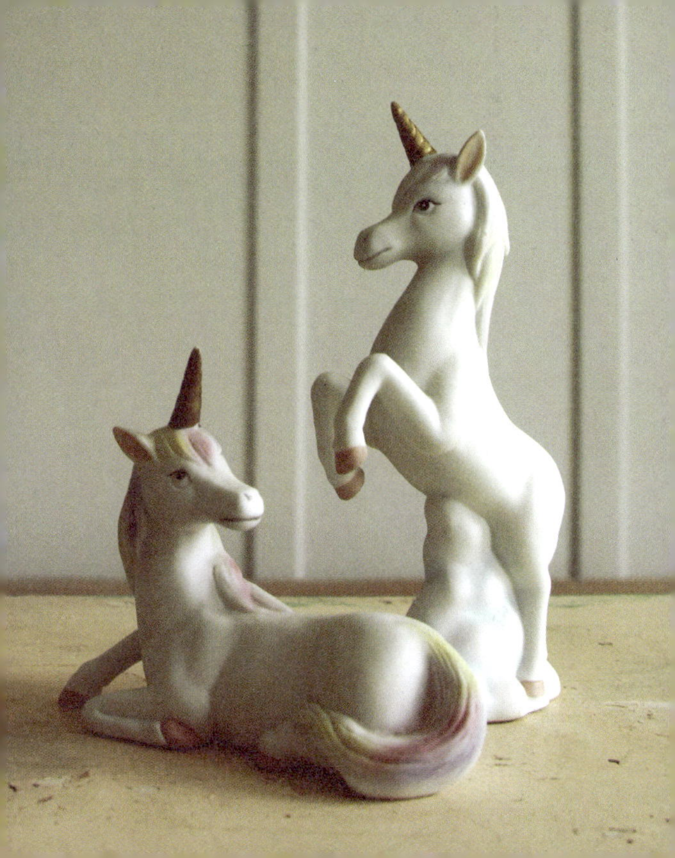

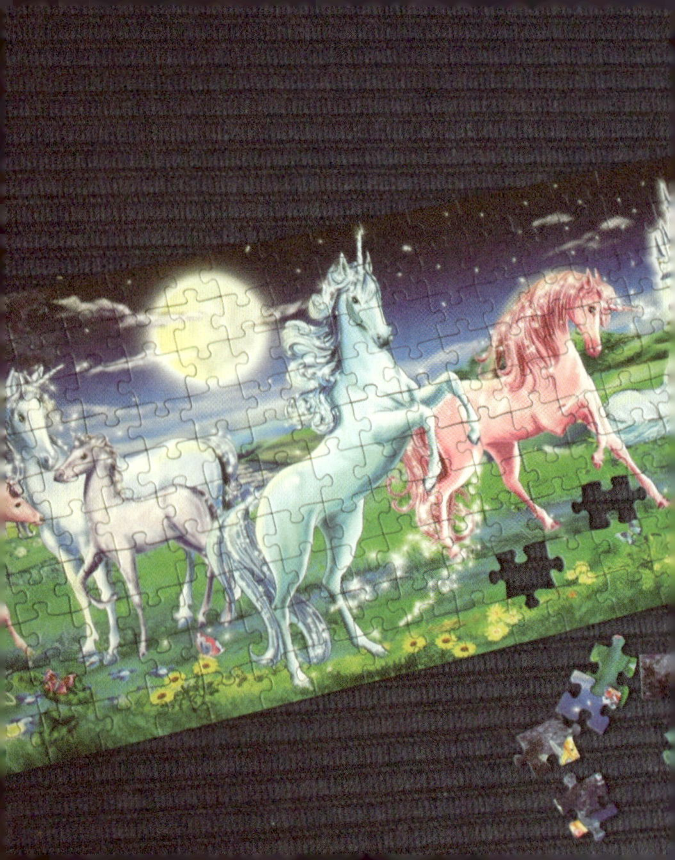

Ravensburger Puzz
200 Panorama

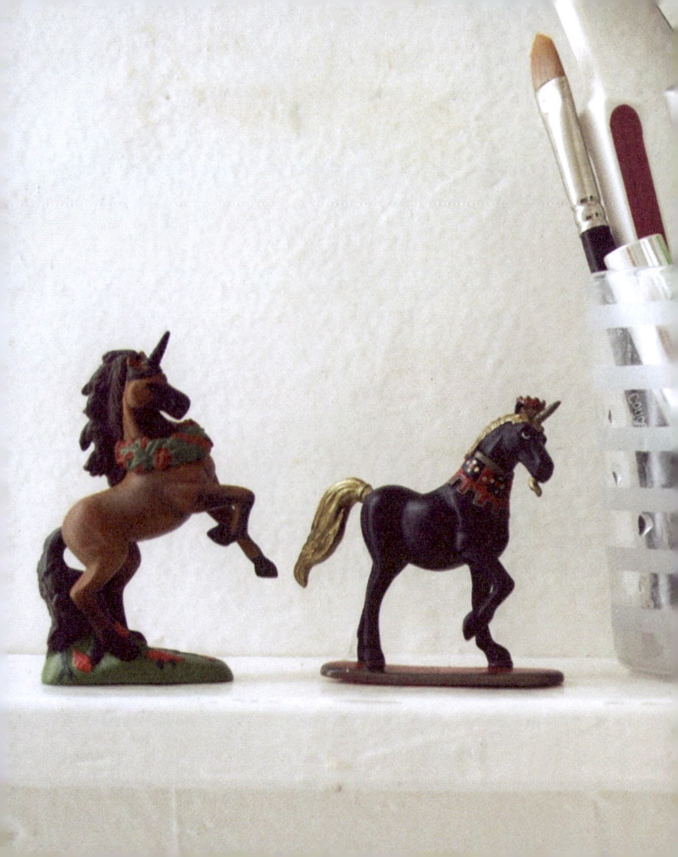

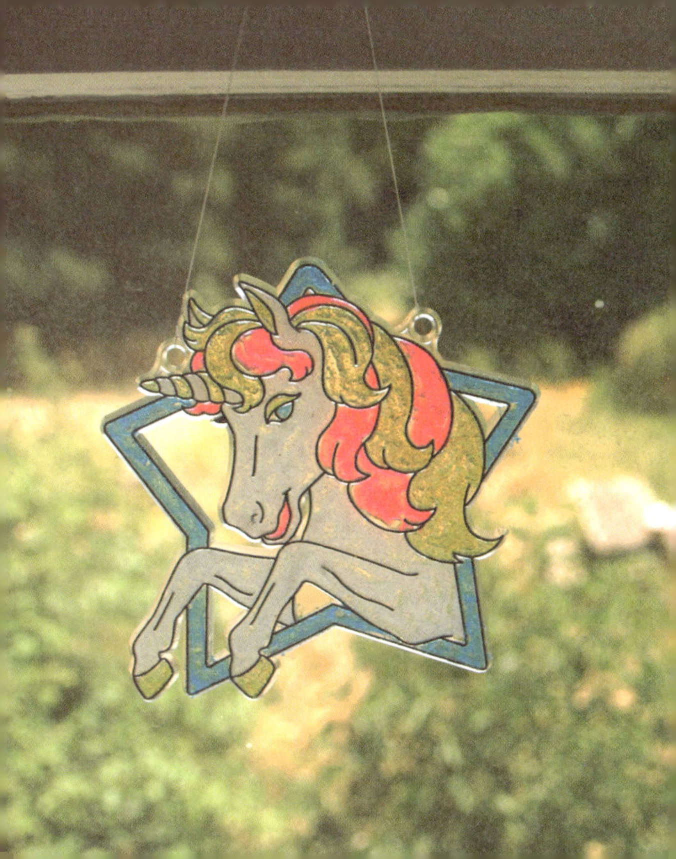

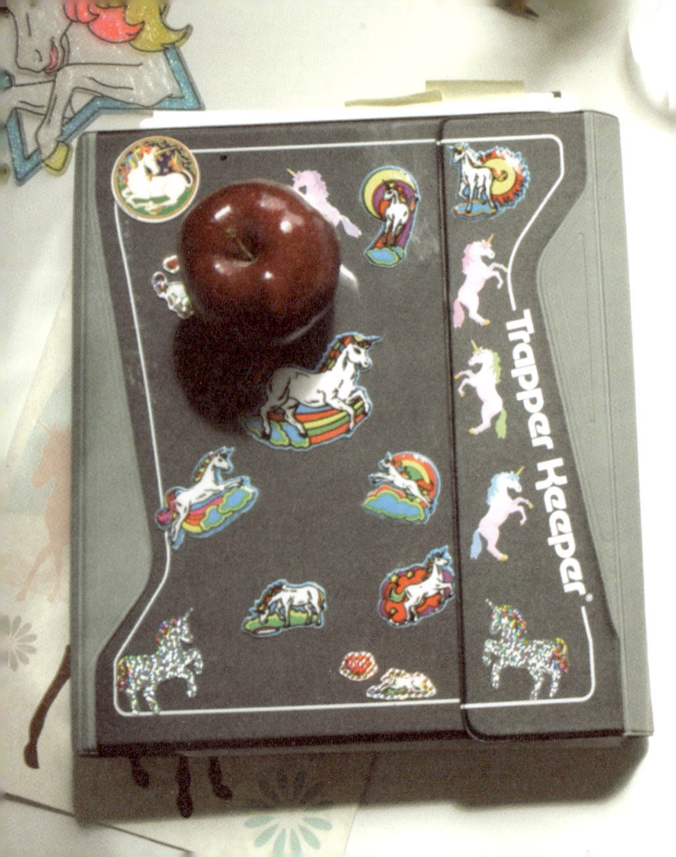
Trapper Keeper®

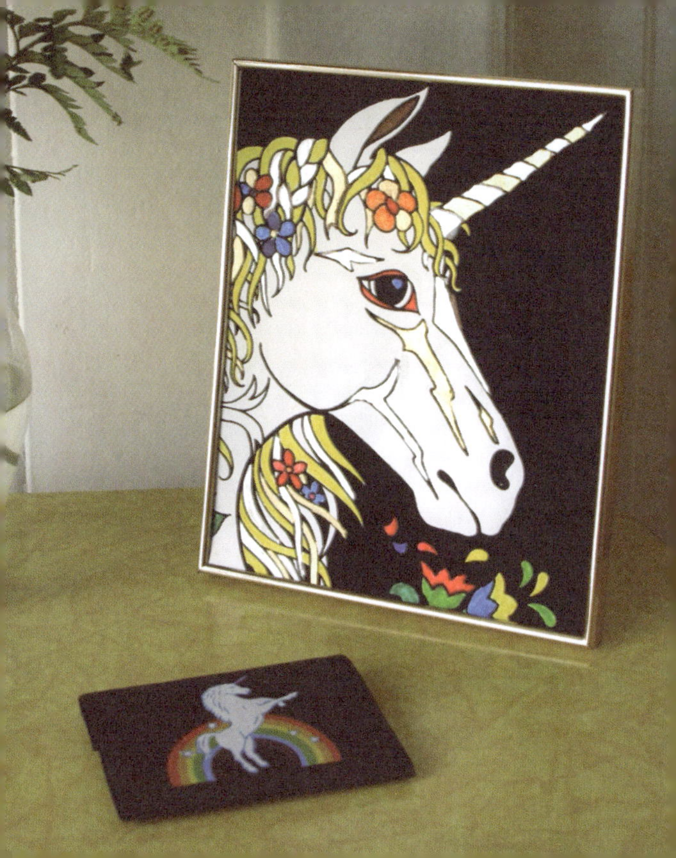

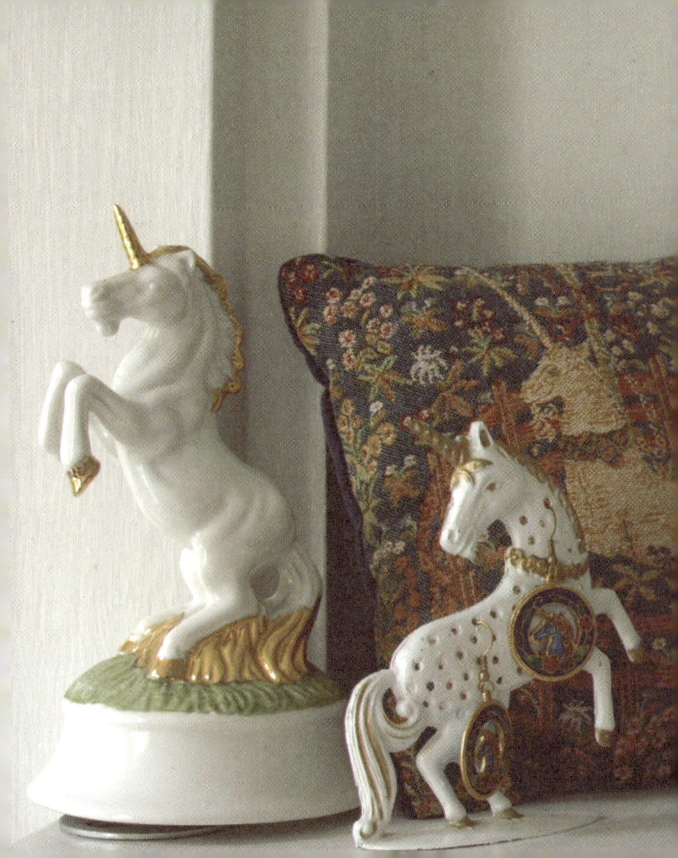

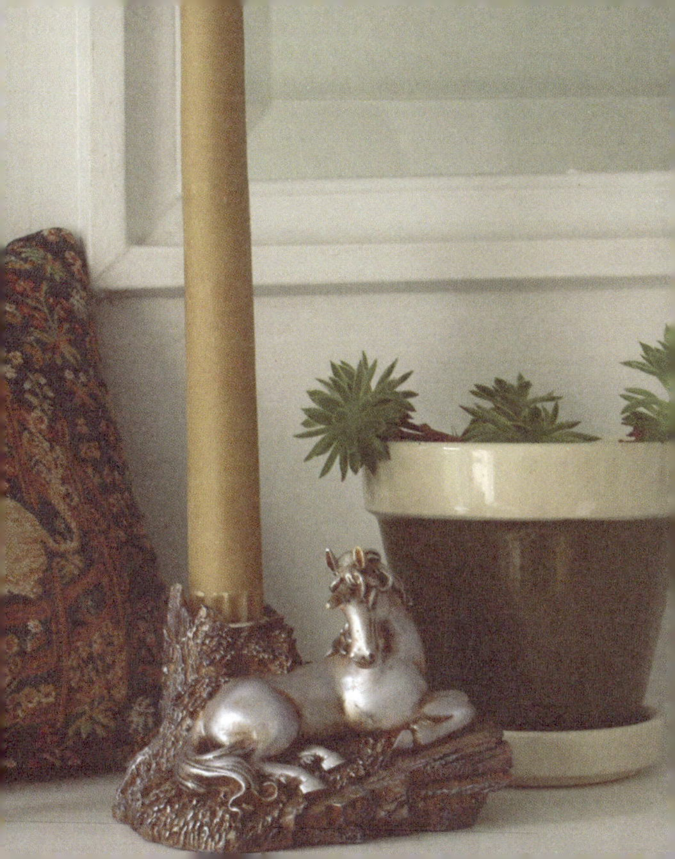

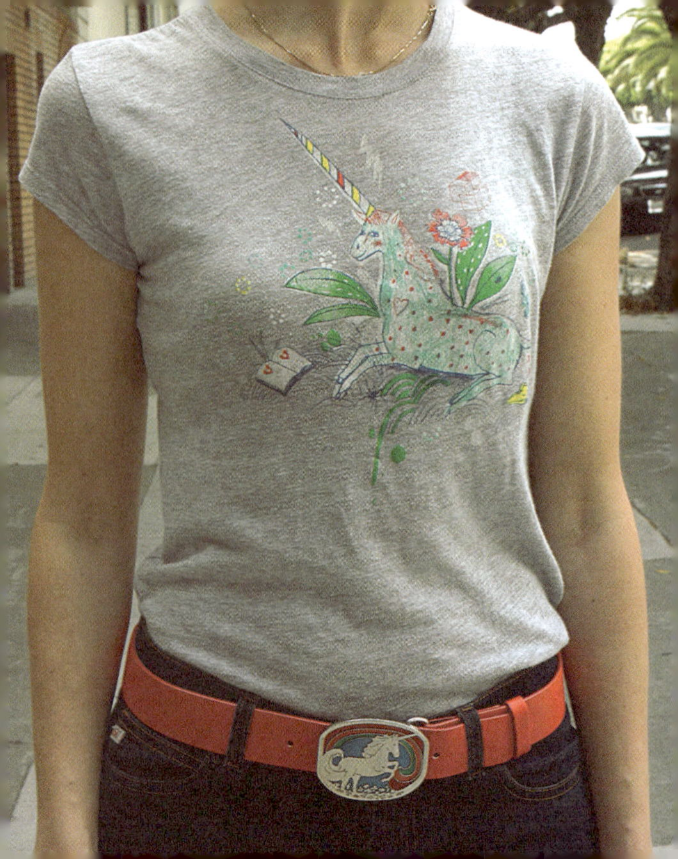

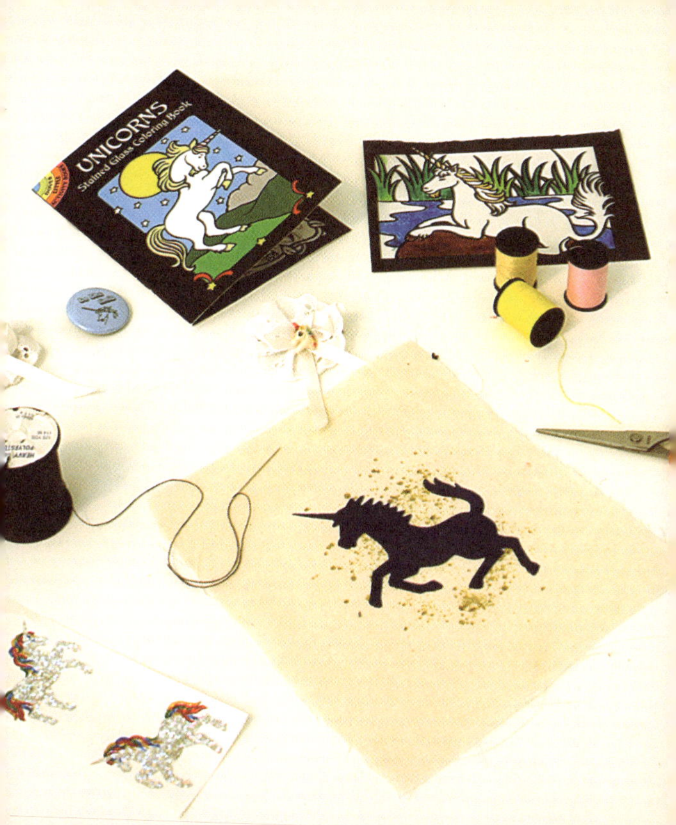
UNICORNS
Stained Glass Coloring Book